i

About the National Science and Technology Council

The National Science and Technology Council (NSTC) is the principal means by which the Executive Branch coordinates science and technology policy across the diverse entities that make up the Federal research and development (R&D) enterprise. One of the NSTC's primary objectives is establishing clear national goals for Federal science and technology investments. The NSTC prepares R&D packages aimed at accomplishing multiple national goals. The NSTC's work is organized under five committees: Environment, Natural Resources, and Sustainability; Homeland and National Security; Science, Technology, Engineering, and Mathematics (STEM) Education; Science; and Technology. Each of these committees oversees subcommittees and working groups that are focused on different aspects of science and technology. More information is available at www.whitehouse.gov/ostp/nstc.

About the Office of Science and Technology Policy

The Office of Science and Technology Policy (OSTP) was established by the National Science and Technology Policy, Organization, and Priorities Act of 1976. OSTP's responsibilities include advising the President in policy formulation and budget development on questions in which science and technology are important elements; articulating the President's science and technology policy and programs; and fostering strong partnerships among Federal, State, and local governments, and the scientific communities in industry and academia. The Director of OSTP also serves as Assistant to the President for Science and Technology and manages the NSTC. More information is available at www.whitehouse.gov/ostp.

About the Subcommittee on Forensic Science

The purpose of the Subcommittee on Forensic Science (SoFS) was to advise and assist the National Science and Technology Council, Committee on Science, and other coordination bodies of the Executive Office of the President on policies, procedures, and plans related to forensic science at the Federal, state, and local levels. The SoFS coordinated a robust effort across Federal, State, and local agencies to identify and address important policy, program, and budget matters, as well as potential activities to enhance and/or amalgamate forensic science initiatives that support research and development; training, education, and ethics; accreditation and certification; and standards of practice. The Subcommittee's findings and work products will inform efforts to enhance future forensic science policy, research, and practice.

Acknowledgements

The SoFS acknowledges the contributions of the following individuals in contributing subject matter expertise and general guidance in support of this effort: Melissa Taylor, Lauren Reed, Robin Jones, Tania Simoncelli, Laura Gerhardt, Terry Green, Mark Greene, Lisa Vincent, Michelle Meder, Anne May, Michael Garris, Martin Herman, Wesley Grose, John Clark, Charles Schaeffer, Michael Lesko, Randy Hanzlick, Leo Norton, Mark Zabinski, Kenneth Blue, Joe Polski, George Kiebuzinski, Peter Komarinski, Rachel Wallner, Austin Hickland, and John Mayer-Splain.

Copyright Information

Table of Contents

Executive Summary

Automated Fingerprint Identification System (AFIS) interoperability will support public safety throughout the United States by ensuring local law enforcement agencies are better able to coordinate their investigative fingerprinting efforts. The Federal Government has a critical role to play in implementing standards needed to achieve interoperability, developing an overarching national connectivity strategy and infrastructure, and supporting State and local agencies in building connections across jurisdictions. This report describes the current state of latent AFIS interoperability and identifies actions that can be taken by Federal agencies to support the following:

- Acquisition of standards-compliant systems at the Federal, State, and local-levels;

- Furthering connectivity efforts among law enforcement agencies;

- Improved governance structures to reflect the new interoperable environment;

- Developing mechanisms to test system performance and standards compliance; and

- Expanded examiner training.

For over a century, fingerprints have been used among other applications to identify criminal and terrorist suspects, perform background checks, and monitor immigration status. In the context of a criminal investigation, prints found at the scene of a crime, known as latent prints, are compared with fingerprint records of known individuals who have been convicted or arrested for a crime. A "latent print" refers to any left fingerprint by an unknown source, in whole or in part, and includes those recovered from a crime scene or an item of evidence. The highly variable characteristics of latent prints complicate the identification process.

When law enforcement first began using fingerprints in investigations, the comparison process was entirely manual and based on visual inspections of features found on both the latent print and the fingerprint records. AFIS systems, first introduced in the 1970s, generate a list of potential candidates that share similar fingerprint features to an encoded image of the print through the use of image recognition algorithms. The algorithms assess friction ridges and other features found on the underside of the finger and on the palm, collectively referred to as "minutiae."

Developers of AFIS software differentiate themselves from their market competitors by creating algorithms that mitigate variations in latent print quality. These proprietary approaches have resulted in insufficient interoperability among different AFIS systems to meet law enforcement's needs.

"Interoperability" is the ability of two or more networks, systems, devices, applications, or components to work seamlessly and electronically without any special effort to share information on demand, when needed, and as authorized without loss of accuracy using standardized encoding. Interoperability of AFIS software would allow law enforcement agencies to search sets of fingerprint records beyond those within their own jurisdictions in support of efforts to identify suspects and protect public safety.

True interoperability requires technical compatibility, network connectivity, proper governance, and performance testing and training within and between systems. A national effort to improve interoperability in order to pursue public safety objectives is underway in each of these areas.

Technical compatibility. Technical compatibility is necessary for interoperability to allow AFIS systems to communicate electronic data. It has been mostly achieved for ten-print searches and is advancing for latent fingerprint searches through the development of standards. Two recent standards that have advanced technical compatibility are the Extended Feature Set (EFS), which defines a common file format and the Latent Interoperability Transmission Specification (LITS), which delineates what information is needed in a transaction between systems.[1] The Federal Bureau of Investigation (FBI) recently introduced the Next Generation Identification (NGI) system, which has incorporated the EFS as the standard submission format for all of its latent print searches. The success of these standards now depends on their adoption by State and local agencies, which is presently underway.

Network connectivity. Law enforcement agencies' coordinated efforts to identify suspects across jurisdictional lines depend on the connectivity of different AFIS systems through established networks. At present, latent print data sharing is relatively limited. State agencies have an AFIS that has direct access to NGI via the Criminal Justice Information Services (CJIS) Wide Area Network (WAN), a network capable of transmitting latent searches to and from the NGI system. Efforts are being explored to connect State agencies to one another and to connect local agencies to NGI through their State Identification Bureau (SIB) for latent searches.

Proper Governance. Proper governance is required for interoperable sharing agreements so that agencies are transparent about their search activities, respect relevant privacy laws, and outline the conditions of cross-jurisdictional data sharing. Interagency coordination has been facilitated by guidelines on the process for developing agreements between agencies and the recommended language for these agreements, but many jurisdictions have not yet pursued agreements.

Performance Testing and Training. Underpinning the effectiveness of an interoperable system is assurance that the examiners are adequately trained and that the software complies with newly adopted standards, provides accurate results, and functions properly. Quality assurance of examiners has improved through the introduction of an online EFS training tool that allows examiners and AFIS vendors to explore the functionality of the EFS.

Education and Outreach. Education and outreach are an important overarching components for bringing about interoperability. Expanding outreach will support other Federal efforts to ensure AFIS interoperability and speed the adoption of standards.

---

[1] U.S. Department of Commerce, National Institute of Standards and Technology (NIST), *Latent Interoperability Transmission Specification*. NIST Special Publication 1152, January 2013, and U.S. Department of Justice, FBI, *Electronic Biometric Transmission Specification (EBTS) Technical and Operational Update (TOU) 10.0.2*, June 2, 2014.

Introduction

This report, *Achieving Interoperability for Latent Fingerprint Identification in the United States,* provides the current landscape of latent Automated Fingerprint Identification System (AFIS) interoperability, outlines recent advances in the field, and provides a high-level strategic plan for Federal agencies to implement the necessary requirements for interoperability to enhance public safety. The report addresses five essential elements of interoperability—technical compatibility, network connectivity, proper governance, performance testing and training, and education and outreach. It also examines existing mechanisms for sharing information and coordinating fingerprint searches and outlines a pathway for building on best practices to achieve a national latent print interoperability infrastructure.

For over a century, fingerprints have been used among other applications to identify criminal and terrorist suspects, perform background checks, and monitor immigration status to support public safety. In the context of a criminal investigation, prints found at the scene of a crime, referred to as latent prints, are compared with fingerprint records of known individuals who have been convicted or arrested for a crime. When law enforcement agencies first began using fingerprints in investigations, the comparison process was entirely manual and based on visual inspections of features found on both the latent print and the fingerprint records.

Law enforcement agencies began working with industry to automate this comparison process in the late 1970s and early 1980s by employing AFISs. After a latent print search has been initiated, an AFIS systems use image-recognition algorithms to generate a list of potential candidates that share similar fingerprint features to an encoded image of a latent fingerprint. The algorithms assess friction ridges and other features found on the underside of the finger and on the palm, collectively referred to as "minutiae." To submit a search, fingerprint examiners manually encode ("markup") an image to indicate the locations of minutiae on a digital image of the print. Law enforcement agencies have benefitted from the adoption of AFIS systems because potential suspects can be identified more quickly and accurately, often when no suspect was developed through other investigative methods.

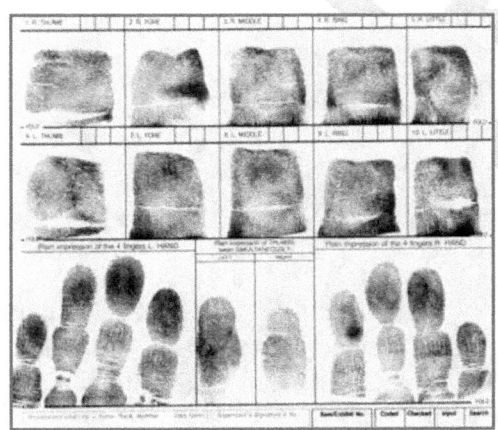

Figure 1. Example of a ten-print record

Law enforcement agencies perform two types of fingerprint identification using AFIS: exemplar searches (more commonly known as "ten-print" searches) and latent print searches. A ten-print record contains fingerprint images of up to ten fingers captured by law enforcement, or private entities in a controlled environment as a result of arrest, conviction, or other civil requirements. Consequently, these images are typically high quality and uniform, resulting in consistency within and across agencies. Ten-print records are used in civil applications such as background checks and to determine immigration status; they are also used in the intelligence arena to identify known or suspected terrorists, and in the criminal justice system to identify perpetrators of crime. Modern AFIS systems use automatic and standardized methods to encode a new ten-print image and search it against existing ten-print records, facilitating fast and accurate searches.

Figure 2. Latent print

By contrast, a "latent print" (Figure 2) refers to any fingerprint, in whole or in part, left by an unknown source, and includes those recovered from a crime scene or other item of evidence. The highly variable characteristics of latent prints complicate the identification process. Latent prints are often incomplete or smudged, as they are usually created in the commission of a crime, not a controlled environment, thus reducing their quality and uniformity. Further chemical and physical processing and photographing or scanning of latent prints may be necessary to visualize the latent print before a search can be run using the image. An AFIS search can introduce additional variations among latent prints that might have been generated from the same individual. When fingerprint examiners perform a latent print AFIS search, they mark up the minutiae features that can be identified on the friction ridges that appear in the image. This process is inherently subjective, and may be vulnerable to human error, especially in cases where the latent print is distorted or smudged or when the examiner is improperly trained or rushed.

Identification of Missing Persons

Fingerprints can be useful in identifying missing persons or victims of mass fatalities. Unidentified, burned, or fragment fingerprints can sometimes be captured and used to make identifications. In some cases, medical examiners and coroners may be able to obtain ten-print records from bodies found at the scene of a crime or recovered from an accident. In other instances, latent searches can be performed on fragmented prints to assist with identification.

Developers of AFIS software have created different methods for encoding features seen in a latent print and algorithms for comparing latent prints to previously recorded ten-print records in order to differentiate themselves from their market competitors. These different approaches have made it difficult for the encoding features used in one vendor system to be used by another vendor system, resulting in insufficient interoperability among different AFIS systems to meet law enforcement's needs.

Defining Interoperability

"Interoperability" is the ability of two or more networks, systems, devices, applications, or components to work seamlessly and electronically without any special effort to share information on demand, when needed, and as authorized without loss of accuracy using standardized encoding.

Email provides a useful analogy for AFIS Interoperability. A user is able to both send and receive emails regardless of whether the recipient is using the same email client software or operating system.

Modern AFIS systems create electronic data that, if standardized, can allow for interoperability. "Interoperability" is the ability of two or more networks, systems, devices, applications, or components to work seamlessly and electronically without any special effort to share information on demand, when needed, and as authorized without loss of accuracy using standardized encoding. Interoperability is essential for law enforcement agencies to effectively investigate crimes and improves their ability to solve more crimes than stand-alone systems because true interoperability allows law enforcement agencies to search latent fingerprints against sets of ten-print records beyond those that are contained in their own databases within their own jurisdiction.

While data sharing is a major component of interoperability, it is not the only criterion that is required for making interoperability possible. True interoperability requires technical compatibility, network connectivity, proper governance, and performance testing and training. It can only be achieved when an examiner can encode a latent fingerprint once and search the desired AFIS databases seamlessly, in accordance with relevant privacy laws, without having to re-encode the print or compromise search accuracy. Latent print examiners should be able to use the same machine for all of their searches and should not have to rely on manual re-encoding of images. This requires an integrated networking of AFIS systems nationally that enables the exchange of fingerprint records to occur on demand, rather than ad hoc.

Progress toward achieving interoperability has been made to date in each of these areas as follows:

- **Technical compatibility** has been mostly achieved for ten-print searches and is advancing related to latent fingerprint searches through the adoption of a common file format, the Extended Feature Set (EFS), and the development of a transaction standard, the Latent Interoperability Transmission Specification (LITS).[2] The Federal Bureau of Investigation (FBI) introduced the Next Generation Identification (NGI) system (described at right), which has incorporated the EFS as the standard submission format and LITS as its transaction standard for all of its latent print searches.

> **Federal Bureau of Investigation: Next Generation Identification**
>
> The FBI's NGI allows access to the Repository of Individuals of Special Concern (RISC), a palm print repository, and access to other Federal biometric databases. Its fingerprint friction ridge feature encoders and matchers represent the latest generation of recognition technology, and the accuracy and speed of the system achieve optimal levels. Additionally, several of the factors that previously limited searches of the Integrated Automated Fingerprint Identification System (IAFIS) have been eliminated or substantially mitigated (e.g., complex and proprietary encoding methods).

- **Network connectivity** and data sharing at present, is relatively limited. State agencies have direct access to NGI via the CJIS WAN, a network designated specifically for transmission of extensive law enforcement information including AFIS searches of FBI records and some local agencies may search NGI without going through their States. Efforts are being explored to connect State agencies to one another and to connect local agencies to NGI through their SIB for latent searches.

- **Proper governance** has been facilitated through interagency coordination and guidelines on the process for developing agreements between agencies and recommended language for the agreements. Few localities have set up regional task groups to improve interoperability within their jurisdictions, but many jurisdictions have not yet pursued such agreements.

- **Performance testing and training** has improved through the introduction of an online Extended Feature Set training tool that allows examiners and AFIS vendors to explore the functionality of EFS.[3] Standardized AFIS performance tests to assess the matching accuracy of natively versus remotely encoded prints are still to be developed.

Despite these efforts, several core challenges to achieving true latent fingerprint interoperability remain. Few agencies have upgraded to systems that comply with the recently developed file format and transmission standards. In the interim, latent fingerprint examiners often forgo additional searches or must manually re-encode their prints on co-located workstations to perform searches on other

---

[2] NIST, *Latent Interoperability Transmission Specification*, and FBI, *EBTS TOU 10.0.2*.

[3] The training tool is available at www.nist.gov/forensics/EFSTrainingTool.

jurisdictions' systems because they do not employ the same vendor to administer their AFIS systems. The re-encoding process can be time consuming and requires additional personnel training. When not

properly addressed these small differences can lead to a missed identification. Given the high volume of latent fingerprint examinations, the time burden resulting from re-encoding dissuades investigators from searching other databases in all but the most high-profile cases. When these additional searches are not performed, fewer matches are made, meaning that relevant suspects may go unidentified.

Figure 3. Encoding latent prints for two different AFIS systems by different vendors

While re-encoding enables limited technical interoperability, seamless data sharing across networks or systems can only occur after adoption of information sharing policies between agencies and co-located workstations and integration of software to re-encode the latent print. Absent these agreements or memoranda of understanding (MOUs) and technical infrastructure, remote searching cannot occur and even partial interoperability cannot exist.

The Case for Latent Print Interoperability

In 2012, 53.2% of violent crimes in the United States went unsolved.[4] While it is not possible to predict what portion of these crimes might be solved as a result of creating a truly interoperable latent AFIS network, it is clear that interoperability would aid investigations of some of them. Further, interoperability would help with investigations of unsolved non-violent crimes where latent prints have been recovered and where individuals have been criminally active in other jurisdictions. AFIS interoperability, if fully implemented for latent prints, would improve the speed and efficiency of broader searches.

Many cross-jurisdictional searches have led to the identification of individuals that would have been missed if the law enforcement agency had searched only records contained in its own AFIS. Latent print examiners investigating a 2008 murder in Detroit, Michigan, searched both the Michigan State AFIS and the IAFIS, but neither system generated a candidate. In 2010, Michigan reached out to the Department of Homeland Security's United States Visitor and Immigrant Status Indicator Technology (US-VISIT) and sent a printed copy of the latent print. US-VISIT responded with a potential match to the print. The person identified by US-VISIT was not on file in either the Michigan State database or IAFIS. This ability to search multiple databases, which was facilitated by data sharing agreements, allowed the Detroit police to identify a suspect in the case. Remote searches have also led to the identification of suspects affiliated with Al-Qaeda, suggesting that interoperability would support both public safety and national security efforts.

The current lack of full interoperability has allowed criminals to remain free, and in some cases, to go on to commit additional crimes. An example that dates back to when the State connectivity to IAFIS was not complete, highlights how these gaps challenge public safety efforts. In the 2002 "DC sniper" case, a series of shootings in the Washington, D.C., metropolitan area resulted in ten fatalities and three critical injuries. A month prior to the sniper shootings, the scene of a homicide and robbery at a liquor store in Alabama produced fingerprints that were searched against the State AFIS, with no match. At the time of the crime, the Alabama laboratory had not implemented a connection to IAFIS, nor did they forward the unknown latent prints from this case. Nearly a month later, the FBI requested the prints following a call from a tip

---

[4]   U.S. Department of Justice, FBI, "Offenses Cleared," *Uniform Crime Report Crime in the United States, 2012*, Fall 2013.

line indicating that the suspected "D.C. sniper" may have been connected to the Alabama crime. The latent prints from Alabama matched prints known to belong to an individual in the Immigration and Naturalization Service (INS) database. This INS search helped lead to the identification and subsequent apprehension of two suspects in the case, but the delay in identification, caused, in part, by the lack of system interoperability, contributed to the loss of life.

Since then, the FBI's NGI system has been improved and intentionally designed to provide State and local law enforcement with the opportunity to conduct a latent fingerprint search by submitting additional information such as photographs, palm prints, and iris patterns. NGI will soon have the capability to combine biometric identifiers as search parameters to increase the accuracy of a search. In this multimodal biometric context, interoperability through the adoption of the national standards will be critically important because the effectiveness of a particular search will depend on jurisdictional utilization and submissions to NGI.

Historical Background of Fingerprinting and the Development of AFIS

Prior to the 1970s, latent fingerprint identification units within law enforcement agencies all relied on a manual and laborious process to search latent fingerprints against ten-print records using the Henry Classification System.[5] This system of visually matching card-cataloged paper records to latent print features of ten-print records was time consuming and often did not result in an identification.

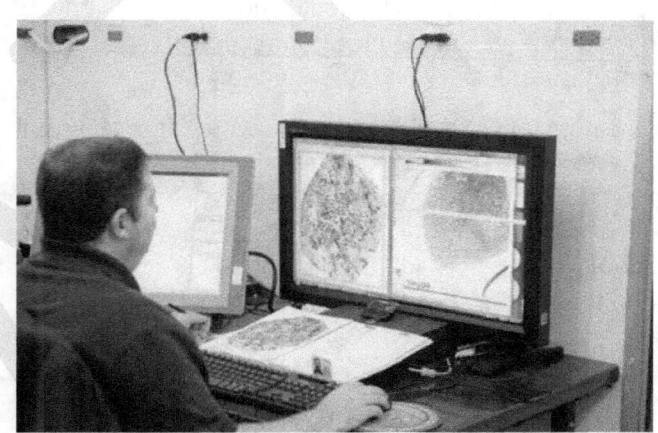

Figure 4. AFIS Workstation

Individual State and local jurisdictions began purchasing AFIS systems in the 1970s and 1980s from various private vendors. Vendors capitalized on the fact that AFIS systems improved the accuracy of identification and dramatically reduced the amount of time necessary to identify or exclude a record from the candidate list by searching against a database of electronic ten-print records of arrested and convicted offenders.[6] AFIS systems also allowed examiners to search both latent and ten-print prints against a greater quantity of ten-print records contained in an AFIS's computerized database.

Each vendor developed their own software and searching algorithms, which, over time, resulted in a stove-piped system of AFIS systems procured throughout the country. AFIS procurements were not coordinated among even geographically close law enforcement jurisdictions, and State policies did not exist that required local agencies to purchase compatible systems. Independent purchasing decisions by agencies from the three major vendors and several smaller vendors created a national system where neighboring jurisdictions and even partners within the same State had vastly different systems. These stove-piped procurements resulted in an inability to automatically share electronic fingerprint data

---

[5] The Henry Classification System was in place through the 1990s, and may still be used today by agencies without AFIS databases.

[6] Early AFIS users continued to use the manual Henry Classification System. In the 1980s, AFIS databases were developed to meet the growing demands for identification and began incorporating functionality to search latent fingerprints against a complete database. This increased capacity became a major selling point to the fingerprint community.

between State and local jurisdictions, even among agencies located in close geographic proximity and more importantly with a shared common criminal pool. This lack of interoperability is in large part due to the lack of industry standards, which lead to variability of vendor specifications and a lack of an integrated network supporting connectivity between two or more jurisdictions. These issues continue to impede crime-solving efforts, and while most AFIS systems are interoperable for ten-print record searches, latent fingerprint interoperability has not been achieved because of the proprietary nature of the encoding schemes integrated into the different AFIS systems.

Efforts in the 1990s supported the development of standards that would enable State systems to communicate with the FBI's IAFIS, the system that preceded NGI. IAFIS became fully operational in 1999 and provided a national system that enabled ten-print records to be shared with the FBI. Through IAFIS, all State-level law enforcement agencies have the capability to submit civil, criminal, and latent prints to the FBI via the CJIS WAN, a collection of Virtual Private Network (VPN) links and near point-to-point T-1 and higher class data lines connecting the FBI CJIS Data Center in West Virginia to selected points throughout the United States and Canada."[7]

In creating IAFIS, the FBI had to accommodate technical limitations at the time of development. Given the low accuracy of optical recognition machine learning at the time, latent examiners had to manually label minutiae and then perform remote searches on already marked up prints, rather than submit unmarked latent prints directly for searching against the system as is currently done in ten-print searching. This re-encoding process had the potential to introduce systematic human errors when the FBI's feature definitions differed from those required by the State or local AFIS. It also decreased the likelihood an FBI search would be made because to perform these extra searches, examiners had to submit images that had been re-encoded to comply with the IAFIS submission requirements, typically through the State.[8]

To standardize submissions to IAFIS (and now to NGI), the FBI required compliance to Electronic Biometric Transmission Specification (EBTS) that has now incorporated the Extended Feature Set (EFS) fingerprint file format.[9] EBTS is based on a standard developed by the American National Standards Institute (ANSI) and the Information Technology Laboratory of NIST (ANSI/NIST-ITL 1-2000). These standards included specifications on image resolution, common field names, and how to include personal information and details on why the fingerprint record was created. More recently, NIST has developed the LITS standard to specify which EFS features are required for latent search submissions.[10]

As more biometric matching capabilities became available, the FBI developed the NGI system. This system expanded the search capabilities and improved speed. Since NGI's adoption 2013, the fingerprinting community has an additional incentive to improve interoperability so that they can take advantage of the significant upgrades to the FBI's system.

---

[7] U.S. Department of Justice, FBI, Privacy Impact Assessment Integrated Automated Fingerprint Identification System (IAFIS)/Next Generation Identification (NGI) Repository for Individuals of Special Concern (RISC), July 10, 2012.

[8] Kenneth R. Moses, Peter Higgins, Michael McCabe, Salil Probhakar, and Scott Swann, "Chapter 6—Automated Fingerprint Identification Systems (AFIS)," *The Fingerprint Sourcebook* (Washington, D.C.: U.S. Department of Justice, 2010: 6-1–33.

[9] When first introduced, EBTS was known as the Electronic Fingerprint Transmission Specification.

[10] NIST, Latent Interoperability Transmission Specification.

Existing Mechanisms for Fingerprint Search Coordination and Sharing in a Tiered and Fragmented System

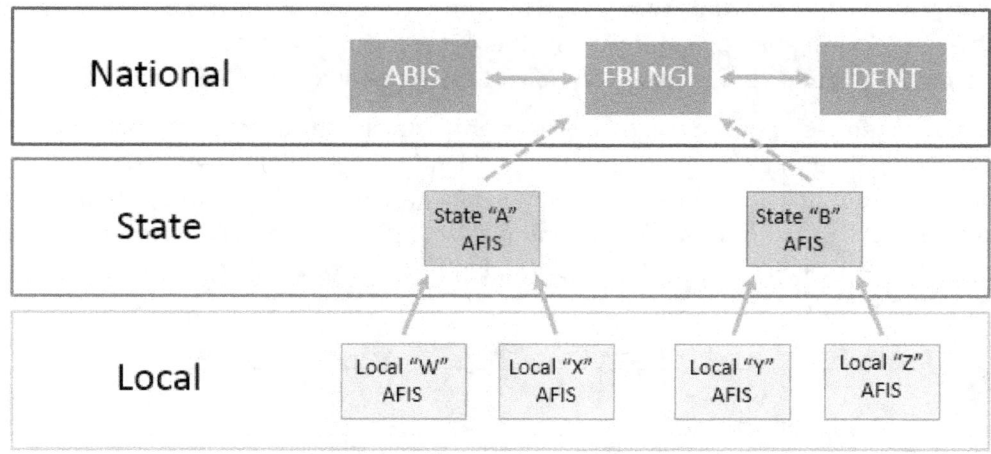

Figure 5. Current AFIS sharing environment

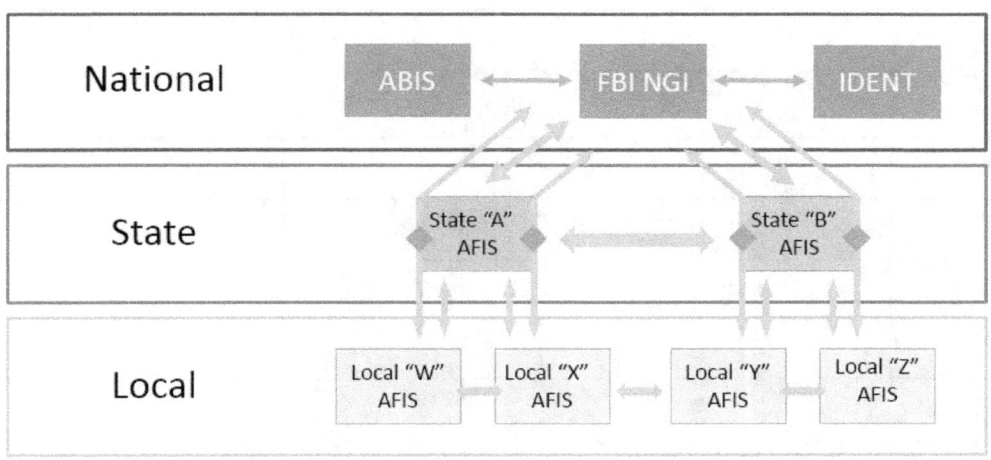

Figure 6. AFIS interoperable environment

The current limited landscape of AFIS interoperability highlights and reinforces the need for interoperability. Multiple tiers of law enforcement agencies perform uncoordinated searches, inhibiting criminal investigations in contrast to an interoperable environment (Figure & Figure 6).

Although built primarily by three major vendors, the majority of the estimated six hundred disparate AFIS systems at the State, local, and Federal level are not interoperable from a technical or governance standpoint. As a result, data sharing is infrequent and case-specific, rather than routine. The sharing that does occur happens primarily through siloed channels in an established hierarchy from local to State and

State to the FBI's NGI. Local law enforcement agencies typically only search their own AFIS, sometimes search their State's AFIS, and rarely share data with neighboring jurisdictions. At the next tier of the hierarchy, State law enforcement agencies rarely submit latent print searches to neighboring States (with the exception of some unique regional agreements). States report low levels of searching against the NGI or neighboring jurisdictions' AFIS databases, even for unsolved cases. While most crimes are solved at the local level and would not require broader sharing, there is some hesitancy to share when appropriate due in part to the limited adoption standards of compliant systems and outmoded examiner practices.

Table 1 highlights agencies' perceptions of their current data sharing levels, and their predicted level of sharing if all of the technical barriers were removed. Significant variability exists among State and local data retention laws and policies.[11] Therefore, innovative governance structures would also need to be introduced to harmonize data retention laws and facilitate data sharing while respecting civil liberties. Without these changes, agencies would have great difficulty conducting an independent search on another local or State AFIS

Table 1. Percentage of Latent Interoperable Searches by Select Jurisdiction

Geographic Area	% Searches Sent to FBI		% Searches Sent to State		% Searches Sent to Neighboring Jurisdictions	
	Current	If Seamless	Current	If Seamless	Current	If Seamless
LOCAL AGENCIES						
Northern Virginia	1%	40–50%	1%	40–50%	80–90%	Already seamless
STATE AGENCIES						
Baltimore, MD*	0%	0%	—	—	0%	0%
Kansas City, MO	10%	20–30%	—	—	0%	20–30%
Michigan	3–5%	100%	—	—	Rarely	100%
New York	80%	80%	—	—	10%	80% (All non-identifications on State AFIS)
REGIONAL AGENCIES						
Portland, OR (Western Identification Network)	15%	20–25%	100%	100%	All non-identifications on State AFIS	All non-identifications on State AFIS
Las Vegas, NV (local AFIS & WIN)	Very rare	All non-identifications on local AFIS	All non-identifications on local AFIS	All non-identifications on local AFIS	All non-identifications on local AFIS	All non-identifications on local AFIS

Source: Noblis, Inc. Latent Print Interoperability: State and Local Perspectives, April 2, 2012.

---

[11] Note that there are multiple reasons beyond interoperability initiatives that result in IAFIS not mirroring other ten-print databases. Many include policy/legal issues in addition to print quality such as lack of data sharing policies.

* Representatives from Baltimore indicated that, given the current latent print examiner staffing level, they could not use interoperability even if it were available.

Sharing at the Local Level

Many cities, counties, and metropolitan areas have independent AFIS that are not interoperable with their own State systems. Most of the local agencies that had their own AFIS databases and responded to a 2013–2014 National Institute of Justice (NIJ) survey on latent fingerprint interoperability reported that they frequently searched their State agencies' data.[12] However, according to State agencies, local agencies in only about half the States forward their unsolved latent prints to State agencies.[13] The survey also found that only 15 States reported that local law enforcement agencies forwarded all unsolved latent prints to the State agency, which is likely due to policy limitations.[14] While some local AFIS are directly connected to the State AFIS, a substantial proportion are not, especially those developed by different vendors.[15] This lack of connectivity weakens the investigative power of the local law enforcement agency, because most State AFIS systems do not contain the sum of all local AFIS data within the State. As a result, suspects who operate in multiple counties may avoid identification.

If local agencies routinely shared fingerprint data among themselves, some of the concerns about the comprehensiveness of the State AFIS's records would be assuaged.

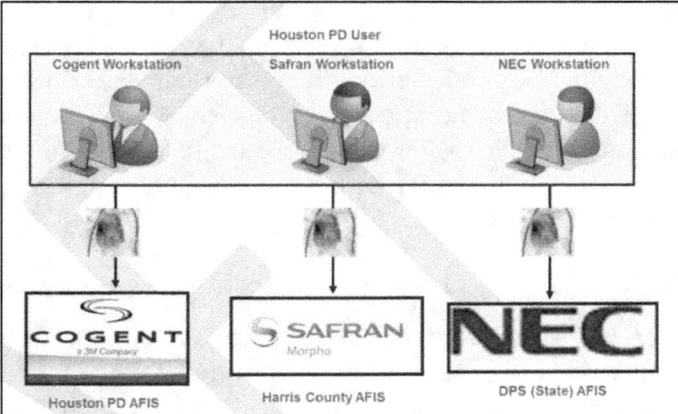

Barriers to Sharing and Interoperability in Houston, Texas

The city of Houston is the largest city in Texas and the fourth-largest in the country. Houston is within Harris County, which is the most populous county in the State and the third-most populous county in the country.

Until recently, Houston and Harris County maintained separate AFIS databases administered by different vendors that were incompatible. The State of Texas also maintained its own AFIS database administered by a third (different) proprietary vendor. For a latent print examiner within Houston Police Department to access the Harris County AFIS database and the Texas State AFIS database, the examiner had to physically access different workstations, each requiring a different method to re-encode the latent print in order to conduct the searches. Now latent fingerprint examiners can utilize the ULW or export a compliant transaction from their proprietary AFIS that can be submitted to the FBI, through DPS, without re-encoding.

---

[12] Mark Persinger, Lars Ericson, and Mark Greene *Latent Fingerprint Interoperability Survey: A National Study of Automated Fingerprint Information Systems (AFIS) Maintained by Law Enforcement Agencies. Summary Reporting of Data Provided by Responding Agencies,* (hereafter referred to as *LFIOS*), (Washington D.C.: Department of Justice, August 2014), Local Addendum Question 28 and State Addendum Question 8.

[13] *LFIOS,* State Addendum Question 8.

[14] *LFIOS,* Question 9.

[15] Among responding local law enforcement agencies, 43% do not have a compatible system with their State AFIS, and only 45% of responding local agencies have an AFIS made by the same vendor as the State. *LFIOS,* Local Addendum Questions 4 and 5. According to Question 1 of the State Addendum of *LFIOS,* the local law enforcement agencies of 14 states do not maintain independent AFIS databases.

But local-to-local sharing is infrequent and especially difficult when neighboring jurisdictions are across State lines. Searching of neighboring AFIS systems is conducted ad hoc and depends on personal relationships among colleagues. Only 19% of responding local law enforcement agencies reported frequent searching of their neighboring jurisdictions.[16] When cross-jurisdictional searches occur, many local agencies prioritize searches by severity of the offense, and 85% of agencies in the NIJ survey who reported prioritizing latent searches based on "criteria associated with the criminal offense under investigation," also reported that "major crimes are prioritized regardless of the jurisdiction" of origin.[17] Law enforcement agencies face similar challenges partnering with other local jurisdictions governing the same geographic region. Some larger municipalities with their own independent AFIS do not have the same AFIS vendor as the county agency and must re-encode latent prints on a separate workstation to search the county AFIS.

State and Local Access to Next Generation Identification

Every State in the Nation has direct access to IAFIS through the CJIS WAN, a dedicated network connecting State and local agencies to the FBI. Further, about 50 local law enforcement agencies are able to directly submit searches through Direct Local Connectivity (DLC). Despite this connectivity, when asked if they ever searched latent prints on IAFIS or NGI, five State agencies reported that they had not, though 31 States responded that they searched IAFIS routinely.[18] This access is primarily through a State law enforcement agency, using separate Universal Latent Workstations (ULW), free software provided by FBI that prepares fingerprint data to be sent to the FBI via the FBI's secure network CJIS-WAN. Among local agencies that reported they submit searches to IAFIS, about half reported submitting them directly and the other half reported submitting them through their State law enforcement agencies.[19] There is a State-level daily query limit for latent searches that exceeds States' current utilization of the system. In Fiscal Year 2014, there were an average of 13,000 remote searches a month. The submission rate influenced by workflow issues that arise from examiners needing to re-encode minutiae because of lack of AFIS interoperability. The need to re-encode makes searching NGI time-consuming and requires additional training. State examiners may also be less likely to pass along local searches to the NGI unless they are relevant to State law enforcement agency investigations.

Regional Interoperability Agreements

According to the NIJ survey, the majority of States (77%) receive latent requests from law enforcement agencies with an AFIS from outside of their State, but just over half described these requests as being routine.[20] Some regions have formalized these sharing relationships to facilitate routine cross-border sharing. Other States have developed bilateral sharing agreements, though these agreements fall short of specifying interoperability (see box). Such agreements often do not support reciprocal sharing and can be invalidated if one agency switches to another AFIS vendor or upgrades to a newer version of their existing vendor's software.

---

[16] *LFIOS*, Local Addendum Question 16.

[17] This figure was consistent across both State and local responding agencies (*LFIOS*, Questions 162 and 63).

[18] While this would suggest that 31 agencies routinely searched NGI at the time of data collection, the FBI was still using IAFIS (*LFIOS*, State Addendum Questions 30 and 31).

[19] *LFIOS*, Local Addendum Question 39.

[20] *LFIOS*, Question 169 and Question 170.

Western Identification Network

The Western Identification Network (WIN) is the most comprehensive regional sharing agreement. Eight western States share a common Automated Biometric Identification System (ABIS) Service Bureau and maintain reciprocal search agreements with the California Department of Justice, Las Vegas in Nevada, and Riverside-San Bernardino counties in California. State WIN agencies that are part of the central service bureau and participating interface agencies have access to more than 30 million fingerprint records and search WIN's AFIS without re-encoding searches. Local agencies can access WIN via a WIN workstation or the through standards-based Universal Latent Workstation (ULW) and ten-print submissions from any authorized workstation. In 2012, there were 7,000 daily ten-print submissions and 500 latent print submissions to WIN.

For agencies that have switched or plan to switch AFIS system vendors, reciprocal search agreements will remain in place and allow agencies to either maintain WIN workstation or use the recently adopted EFS standard accessed via the ULW. Regional connectivity continues to be supported by maintaining a dedicated WIN workstation or implementing ULW software or rapid-standards-based ten-print searches. The WIN workstation supports full system capability (e.g., registration, archive access, latent case management, etc.), while the ULW only supports searching WIN's database.

Regional systems such as WIN and the Northern Virginia Regional Identification System (NOVARIS) have successfully implemented data sharing agreements. These arrangements reveal the benefits and difficulties of full-scale interoperability. Largely, the interactions among the members in these systems have developed in areas where law enforcement agencies shared common vendor or co-located workstations. Unique contractual agreements — usually an MOU that has been developed with the help of the incumbent vendor — have formalized data sharing. If an agency within the network were to change vendors, the data sharing mechanism would likely be broken, because most of these agencies have not yet implemented the data sharing standards necessary for interoperability. Smaller regional interoperability agreements have also been implemented across the United States. [21] Like larger sharing networks, these can be jeopardized if an agency changes its vendor.

Fingerprint Sharing among Federal Systems

At the Federal level, three agencies maintain AFIS systems that are semi-interoperable with one another. The FBI has recently transitioned to the Next Generation Identification (NGI) system that operates in parallel with two other national fingerprinting databases. The Department of Homeland Security (DHS) maintains the Automated Biometric Identification System, called IDENT, a program of the Office of Biometric Management (Figure 7).[22] Latent interoperability between NGI and IDENT is limited, as DHS must re-encode latent prints received from NGI for search in IDENT to ensure the highest level of search accuracy within IDENT in the absence of EFS adoption by DHS. These re-encoding burdens restrict the number of searches that can be searched between the two systems based on manpower and manual throughput. The Department of Defense (DOD) also maintains the Automated Biometric Identification System (ABIS). As of December of last year, DOD ABIS achieved compliance with FBI's standard for ten-print submissions, but has not yet done so for latent prints. In practice, DOD latent print submissions to

---

[21] Kansas Bureau of Investigation, New Hampshire, Vermont, North and South Dakota, Minnesota, Connecticut, Rhode Island, Las Vegas, and other jurisdictions have also employed regional interoperability approaches.

[22] The Office of Biometric Management was formerly known as United States Visitor and Immigrant Status Indicator Technology.

NGI, and NGI latent print submissions to DOD ABIS, are performed by an internal translation system that converts DOD encoded prints into NGI compliant submissions and vice versa.

The connections between States and these Federal agencies primarily occur through NGI. While most States routinely search NGI, only six States have ever directly requested a latent print search from another Federal agency database, only one State is directly connected to other Federal systems, and three others connect through NGI.[23]

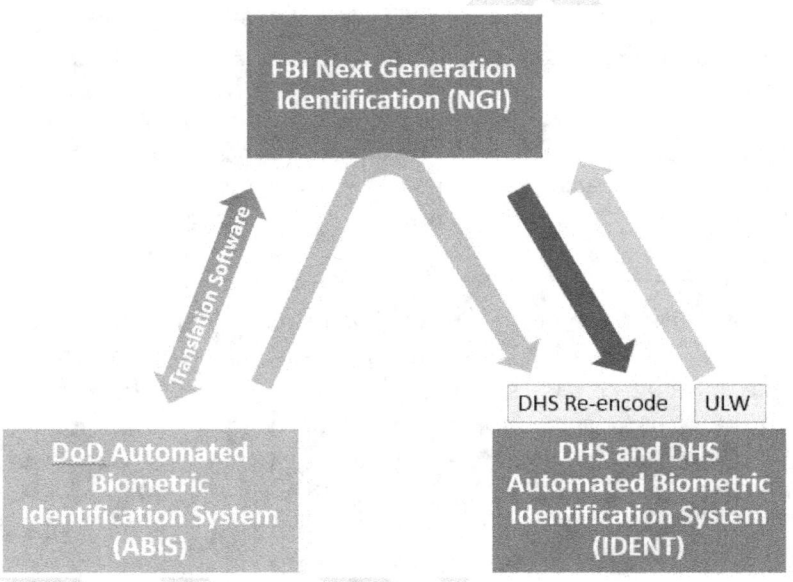

Figure 7. Interoperability among Federal agencies

DHS's Automated Biometric Identification System (IDENT)

IDENT is the central DHS-wide system for storage and processing of biometric and associated biographic information for national security, law enforcement, immigration and border management, intelligence, and other DHS mission-related functions. IDENT was originally developed in 1994 for the Immigration and Naturalization Service (INS). With the incorporation of the INS into DHS in 2002, the use of IDENT was expanded to be DHS's primary biometric identification system. Today, IDENT helps DHS meet many of its statutory requirements under the "Uniting and Strengthening America by Providing Appropriate Tools Required to Intercept and Obstruct Terrorism (USA PATRIOT) Act of 2001,[24] the Homeland Security Act of 2002,[25] the

---

[23] *LFIOS,* State Addendum Questions 51 and 54.

[24] The USA PATRIOT Act of 2001 (P.L. 107-56) required the Attorney General and the FBI to make available to the Department of State and the Immigration and Naturalization Service (now the U.S. Citizenship and Immigration Services) records for determining whether or not a visa applicant or applicant for admissions has a criminal history.

[25] The Homeland Security Act of 2002 (P.L. 107-296) required DHS to oversee and coordinate DHS programs for and relationships with State and local governments.

Enhanced Border Security and Visa Reform Act of 2002,[26] and the Intelligence Reform and Terrorism Prevention Act of 2004.[27] IDENT holds over 170 million individuals' fingerprints provided by DHS agencies such as Immigrations and Customs Enforcement (ICE), Customs and Border Protection (CBP), United States Citizenship and Immigration Services (USCIS), Transportation Security Administration (TSA), and the United States Coast Guard (USCG), as well as other Federal agencies. In addition, IDENT contains over 220,000 latent prints. In contrast to most cross-jurisdictional submissions where latent re-encoding is required, DHS will re-encode a latent print upon receipt as opposed to requiring the submitting agency to re-encode the print to ensure the highest level of search accuracy within IDENT. The need to re-encode could be eliminated if the DHS were to adopt the EFS standard.

DOD Automated Biometric Identification System (ABIS)

The Biometrics Identity Management Activity (BIMA), which falls under the Defense Forensics and Biometrics Agency in DOD, operates the authoritative multimodal biometric database known as ABIS. What began in 2004 as a suite of technologies for securing access to military installations, thereafter became recognized by warfighters as innovative tools for identifying and tracking known or suspected terrorists. For example, in Iraq and Afghanistan, the data contained in ABIS help counter the threat of improvised explosive devices by tracing latent fingerprints back to those who made or detonated these weapons.

In 2009, DOD extended the capabilities of ABIS to include face and iris matching, which, when combined with fingerprint data, reduce response time and human intervention and increase identification accuracy. The ABIS database currently contains more than 12 million biometric files and over 250,000 unsolved latent prints collected from military theaters of operation. In support of homeland security, BIMA shares ABIS data with NGI and IDENT. When the ABIS latent print data is forwarded to IDENT, a team of latent print examiners must start over with the latent print and re-encode it to search the IDENT system. Latent print data forwarded to NGI goes through an automated conversion process that lets it search NGI without an additional human intervention.

Interoperability Pilot Programs

Several pilot programs seek to provide local law enforcement agencies with direct access to NGI and other Federal AFIS systems. By providing an interoperability solution to localities, the capabilities offered by Federal databases can be used more effectively for specific investigatory purposes. These pilots also serve to demonstrate the value of interoperability and mitigate challenges by identifying potential technical and operational solutions.

---

[26] The Enhanced Border Security and Visa Entry Reform Act of 2002, (P.L. 107-173) required an interoperable law enforcement and intelligence data system, and the ability to update IDENT as a critical watch list with known and suspected terrorist information.

[27] The Intelligence Reform and Terrorism Prevention Act of 2004, (P.L. 108-458) required creation of an information sharing environment to share terrorism information across the homeland security, law enforcement, and intelligence communities at all levels of government and the private sector, and accelerated development of an integrated electronic biometric entry-exit screening system (i.e., the Entry/Exit system).

Latent Interoperability Pilot Program

In an effort to expand the availability of latent fingerprint services of DHS's IDENT, DHS and the Texas Department of Public Safety (TXDPS) are developing a Letter of Intent that would permit TXDPS to electronically submit searches to IDENT. Once the agreement is finalized, TXDPS will be able to use existing connectivity provided by the CJIS-WAN to electronically search DHS's IDENT, as TXDPS now does with the ABIS and NGI. Current searches submitted to DHS by TXDPS are done so by non-electronic means. The pilot will help evaluate IDENT's expanded latent print services and its value to the greater law enforcement community at the local level, especially in jurisdictions along the U.S. border.

Other National Pilots for Latent Interoperability

Recent initiatives have targeted introducing latent search capabilities to new users that might benefit from fingerprint identification. These initiatives have allowed the following users to have access to AFIS systems:

- Medical examiners and coroners (ME/C);
- Customs and border protection agents; and
- Patrol officers attempting to identify subjects with fingerprints of reduced quality.

Mobile handheld fingerprint scanning devices that have access to an AFIS database have introduced the possibility of these users incorporating fingerprint identification into their investigations and duties. Most of the data captured by these mobile devices is searched using an automated ten-print or two-print identification process. But some subjects, such as decedents and individuals whose fingerprints are collected in less than ideal conditions, can result in poor quality fingerprint images and require the ability to search using latent fingerprint encoding methods to enhance accuracy. Once these are properly encoded, there may be a need to search multiple databases to identify the individual.

> **AFIS Searches at the Medical Examiner's Office**
>
> A Harris County, Texas, morgue employee used a mobile scanner (and a traditional table-top model) in an attempt to identify and confirm the identification of decedents. The use of the mobile device greatly facilitated the fingerprint capture process, allowing the non-expert to scan all fingers. After receiving the scanned prints, the Harris County Sheriff's Department AFIS database searched for a match and, if available, returned mug shots for identity confirmation. Several identifications against the unsolved latent fingerprint database maintained by Harris County were also obtained as a result of this project.

In most cases, ME/C offices do not have direct authority to access a local jurisdiction's AFIS and must go through a law enforcement agency to perform a search, which impedes their ability to identify decedents. Several pilot programs have placed AFIS workstations and the proper governance in place in ME/C offices to allow them to search the ten-print records maintained at the local or State level.

To achieve interoperability and to take advantage of the information contained in different AFIS databases, changes in laws and policies governing access will need to be considered, and special provisions may need to be included in MOUs established between jurisdictions to allow for access by ME/C and other authorized persons outside law enforcement agencies.

Recent Progress toward Interoperability

Technical Compatibility through the Establishment of Standards

Many interoperability problems arose out of the variability and proprietary nature of individual agencies' AFIS systems encoding specifications for latent prints. In particular, minutiae used for identification in one vendor's AFIS might be unreadable or irrelevant to another AFIS. NIST and ANSI worked extensively to establish a standard set of friction ridges and other minutiae that must be included to search other systems. The EFS standard provides comprehensive and consistent definitions of minutiae for use in fingerprinting. It also specifies methods for encoding features found on fingerprints and palm prints as well as how to annotate the quality of the feature.

In addition, NIST and ANSI specified which EFS features need to be incorporated to submit or receive a remote search regardless of which vendor made the systems. This vendor-neutral transaction standard is known as the Latent Interoperability Transmission Standard (LITS). Since its incorporation into the fingerprint and biometric ANSI/NIST-ITL 1-2011 Update: 2013 standard, there has been mixed success in adoption of the feature set and transmission standard by vendors because localities are not making it a requirement of the contractual agreements with their AFIS vendor. Long-term procurement cycles also make it difficult to update all of the AFIS. In a 2013–2014 survey, the average State and the average local agency reported that their AFIS was upgraded or became operational in 2008.[28] Over 60% of

> **EFS and LITS**
>
> The EFS standard provides comprehensive and consistent definitions of minutiae for use in fingerprinting. This standard defines the features to be used in both ten-print and latent print searches.
>
> The LITS standard describes what information is required for a latent print search transaction to occur across jurisdictions, regardless of originating and destination AFIS system vendor.

States have reported that they plan to update their system or release a procurement announcement for a completely new AFIS in the next 3 years, which presents a unique opportunity to influence the procurement process.[29]

Transition to Next Generation Identification

The FBI's transition to the NGI incorporates functionality that will benefit the latent print examiner community. By implementing the recently adopted standards, NGI will create a more formal channel for local agencies to submit searches to the system and will add palm prints and other biometric identifiers such as facial and iris recognition into records, which will likely increase search and identification accuracy. In early 2013, as part of the third increment of NGI implementation, latent print functionality was migrated from IAFIS to NGI. The new system allows for faster searches, a simplified and standardized encoding process, and the ability to prioritize most pressing searches.

NGI permits latent print examiners to search against the entire criminal database or a particular subset of records such as the Repository of Special Concern (RISC).[30] For example, law enforcement can submit a search to the RISC from remote locations, such as during a traffic stop, with a small handheld device to quickly identify high-interest individuals. Officers are notified of a match probability for each potential candidate in the RISC, using a stoplight color-coded system, (red, yellow, and green). Searches submitted to RISC are also cascaded (automatically searched) against the Unsolved Latent File (ULF), a group of unsolved cases.[31] Thus, this setup may help identify suspects in cold cases. Unlike ten-prints in the RISC system, the ULF search does not immediately return the personal information of a hit. Instead, RISC only

---

[28] For States and local agencies that responded that they had upgraded their systems (*LFIOS*, Question 25), this average counted the year they had upgraded (Question 26). For those who had not upgraded their AFIS, the average counted year the system became operational (*LFIOS*, Question 11).

[29] *LFIOS*, Question 24 and Question 35.

[30] When authorized, examiners may search latent prints against civil records.

[31] James J. Landon, Privacy Impact Assessment Integrated Automated Fingerprint Identification System (IAFIS)/Next Generation Identification (NGI) Repository for Individuals of Special Concern (RISC), Federal Bureau of Investigation, July 10, 2012.

notifies and forwards potential candidates to the examiner for verification when a possible hit is generated. RISC contains only a subset of NGI's records.

Beyond some of the technical limitations that still remain with NGI, the overall challenge with the transition to NGI is the limited capacity of latent examiners to run an additional search in the NGI system or compare the resulting candidate lists. A number of States do not routinely submit searches to NGI due to time and resource constraints.

Improving Latent Print Algorithms

While vendor competition has stymied collaboration and cross-jurisdictional compatibility, it has encouraged vendors to strive for more accurate search algorithms. Advances in latent print identification algorithms have allowed latent print examiners to identify more suspects, especially with poor quality prints due to increased accuracy of the search. Vendors are also starting to use ensemble methods to bundle multiple search algorithms to generate candidate lists.

These recent technical advances have allowed law enforcement to work towards building an interoperable system capable of quickly and efficiently solving more crimes. Much more needs to be done to bring the system from a fragmented system of ad hoc sharing to one that is fully interoperable. The next section provides a path forward from the current landscape to an interoperable latent print system. It is possible that at some point, these search algorithms will become so refined in their ability to read latent print images that they may eliminate the need for human encoding in most cases, which would likely speed up the latent print search process. Improved encoding, while speeding up the submission process, does not eliminate the need for the examiner to compare candidate lists returned as a result of a particular search.

Path Forward: Essential Elements for Interoperability

An alternative to the current multiple AFIS databases would be a system whereby all law enforcement agencies in the United States submit every latent print to a central repository of biometric information, within the bounds of standardized privacy laws. Ideally, this system would be a single interface that accesses all law enforcement systems, allowing users to select to run a search against a local, state, or national database, when appropriate. Such a system could provide seamless technical compatibility, network connectivity, a comprehensive governance framework that ensures secure transfers and respects privacy laws, and rigorous quality assurance mechanisms for both technology and staff that use and manage the system.

Maintaining a centralized system would likely be infeasible given the cost of procurement and retraining and logistical concerns of connecting every law enforcement agency. The elements necessary to maintain an effective single system are the same as those in an environment of distinct interoperable systems.[32] Additionally, education and outreach are necessary to promote the advances in these other areas. The Federal Government and State and local agencies have made varying progress on implementing these elements. The following sections define the requisites for each component, enumerate progress that has been made toward incorporating each element, identify outstanding challenges, and provide recommendations to address these challenges.

Technical Compatibility

Interoperability depends on the technical compatibility of electronic data submitted and received between two or more agencies' software systems. In the context of latent print searches, compatibility requires consistent fingerprint feature definitions, and designating a minimum set of features that must be encoded on the digital image to conduct a latent print search. These "feature sets" allow for latent prints to be compared to both ten-print records and other latent print records that exist within an AFIS.

The AFIS market has always been competitive and has multiple vendors who successfully marketed their products to different law enforcement agencies. Engineers from different vendors built systems that had varying algorithms that define requirements for identifying and weighting the features of a latent fingerprint image. In response to the requirements specified in law enforcement agencies' requests for proposals (RFPs), engineers prioritized accuracy and ease-of-use within a single AFIS, instead of compatibility with other AFIS. Vendors, furthermore, often did not include legacy compatibility, thus making newer AFIS systems incompatible with older versions from the same vendor.

Recent Progress on Compatibility and Remaining Challenges

Recognizing the need for compatibility, the Committee to Define an Extended Fingerprint Feature Set (CDEFFS),[33] composed of a broad spectrum of stakeholders, including law enforcement officials, latent

---

[32] An environment of distinct systems may encourage better search algorithms through vendor competition. Models, however, that directly encourage vendors to compete for a single procurement such as those employed by the Indian Government may be especially effective at spurring advancing AFIS accuracy.

[33] At the ANSI/NIST ITL 1-2000 Standard Workshop I in April 2005, the Scientific Working Group on Friction Ridge Analysis, Study, and Technology (SWGFAST) was tasked to identify, define, and provide guidance on additional fingerprint features beyond the traditional ending ridges and bifurcations defined in the ANSI/NIST ITL 1-2000 standard. (NIST, *NIST Special*

fingerprint examiners, academics, and engineers from major AFIS vendors, set out to establish a features encoding standard to be incorporated in the 2013 update of the ANSI/NIST-ITL 1-2011 standard. The result was the EFS, which created standardized minutiae and friction ridge feature definitions and standardized data field names and indexing. This updated standard defines the features to be used in both ten-print and latent print searches and is consistent with the FBI's broader biometric standard, the Electronic Biometric Transmission Standard (EBTS). EBTS has been incorporated in major systems including NGI and systems of INTERPOL and DOD.[34] NIST testing of the EFS has demonstrated that it provides the basis for a common set of features that all major vendors can use.[35]

Building on this standard, the NIST Law Enforcement Standards Office, now the Office of Special Programs Forensic Science Program, developed the LITS specification document that describes what information is required for a search across jurisdictions.[36] LITS requires that latent print submissions include transactional meta-data, the latent print image, and minutiae data. By incorporating LITS directly into the local and State AFIS, law enforcement agencies will reduce the need to encode latent prints on multiple workstations. In doing so, it will remove many of the technical and workflow barriers that limit fingerprint data sharing and interoperability today.

The LITS designates two different sets of features called "profiles" to be interoperable across all systems: the image-only search and the quick minutiae search.[37] These profiles are vendor-neutral and can be used across systems that have adopted the LITS. Additional information can be encoded to be used by specific vendors or future systems by submitting additional markup details through set profiles (Table 2). The additional profiles may allow examiners to increase their accuracy by encoding additional features, including vendor-specific features. Examiners have to weigh the tradeoff between encoding additional features and utilizing that time to perform comparisons or to search additional databases.

Publication 500-245: Data Format for the Interchange of Fingerprint, Facial, & Scar Mark & Tattoo (SMT) Information, ANSI/NIST-ITL 1-2000. July 2000).

[34] NGI interoperability is ensured because the LITS is compliant with the EBTS, which includes specifications for many biometric modalities. EBTS specifications may be found at www.fbibiospecs.org/ebts.html.

[35] NIST also developed resources instructing examiners how to properly annotate features using EFS, including the Extended Feature Set Training Tool found at http://www.nist.gov/forensics/EFSTrainingTool/TrainingTool.html.

[36] For the full specification see noblis.org/media/d58f0f47-37b9-4ea2-81c5-ab5a6972f62f/docs/LITS_v1-0_2012-02-15_pdf and nvlpubs.nist.gov/nistpubs/SpecialPublications/NIST.SP.1152.pdf.

[37] Image-only searches can be supplemented with a minimal markup profile for the purposes of defining a region of interest, orientation, finger/palm print position, pattern class, cores, and deltas.

Table 2. EFS Profiles that are required by LITS and optional additional EFS profiles supported by LITS

LITS Required		LITS Optional
Latent Image-Only Search	**Quick Minutiae Search**	**Detailed Markup Profile**
The image is properly cropped and submitted without markup or annotations.	The latent print examiner must mark region of interest, minutiae, cores, deltas, pattern, and orientation.	Ridge Flow Map is one of the features included as part of the detailed profile.

Source: Austin Hicklin, *Standardizing a More Complete Set of Fingerprint Features*, (Noblis, Inc., 2007), prepared for the Committee to Define to an Extended Feature Set. Screen taken shot from EFS Training Tool www.nist.gov/forensics/EFSTrainingTool/FundamentalAFISSearching/MarkingMinutiae.html.

Incorporation of the LITS is ongoing and vendors are beginning to build systems that natively use the EFS features and profiles defined by LITS. To support the adoption of LITS-compliant systems, NIST has developed writing guidelines for agencies to use in preparing their RFPs.[38] As of September 2014, few law enforcement agencies had purchased LITS-compliant workstations because upgrades are both costly and require substantial training of print examiner staff. Of those law enforcement agencies who responded to the recent NIJ survey and reported having upgraded their systems, the last upgrade occurred on average 6 years ago for State agencies and 5 years ago for local agencies, prior to the adoption of the LITS standard.[39] While over two-thirds of responding State agencies reported that they expected a major upgrade of their systems within the next 3 years,[40] only 35% of responding local agencies expected a major upgrade within that timeframe.

In the interim, a small subset of law enforcement agencies are using the ULW to support their interoperability needs. The ULW software is freeware provided by the FBI that can run on most computers and that has been updated to allow the examiner to encode using the interoperable LITS format. Most

---

[38] Latent Print AFIS Interoperability Working Group. *Writing Guidelines for Requests for Proposals for Automated Fingerprint Identification Systems.* National Institute of Standards and Technology, February, 17 2012.

[39] As mentioned in the previous section, the estimated average age of the AFIS is approximately 6 years old. (*LFIOS*, Question 25).

[40] *LFIOS*, Question 35.

states currently receive all search results from the FBI through the ULW.[41] Many vendors have not incorporated export or translation functionality to ULW. Without this functionality, latent examiners must manually re-encode prints to submit them to NGI. Half of States currently re-encode prints prior to submitting a search to the FBI.[42]

The existence of biometric standards alone is not enough to demonstrate that an AFIS system meets the technical requirements specified in the standards. Conformance testing is also necessary to ensure LITS compliance. Information on an AFIS system's conformance to a particular standard can provide an efficient method of conveying information on the product's suitability. Conformance testing, which captures the technical description of a specification and measures whether the specification has been faithfully implemented, have yet to be developed for LITS and EFS. Future tests should evaluate the data structure (syntactical conformance), the data content and relationships between fields (morphological conformance), and whether the data represent the parent biometric data (semantic conformance).

Path Forward for Compatibility and Compliance

The Federal Government could take several steps to help speed the adoption of LITS-compliant AFIS systems and ensure compliance to newly implemented standards. First, the Committee members believe the Federal Government should set a clear example by ensuring that all Federal AFIS systems are made fully LITS compliant without the use of an additional workstation within 3 years. Next, the Federal Government should provide support to State and local agencies through existing grant programs for achieving LITS compliance.

Federal funds could be made available to State and local agencies for AFIS procurement or upgrades, provided the systems are LITS-compliant. Finally, NIST should ensure that the recently adopted standards are appropriate once implemented and are reviewed in 3 years. NIST could also ensure that updates to the ANSI/NIST ITL 1-2011 are backward-compatible and provide guidance on how to improve interoperability with legacy system, while agencies upgrade their systems in the interim.

In order to validate LITS-compliance, NIST should develop conformance testing standards to assess the incorporation of the ANSI/NIST-ILT, EFS, EBTS, and LITS standards into new AFIS systems. NIST could either develop a conformance testing program or fund independent programs that assess an AFIS system's compliance to these standards (See text box on Recommended Criteria for Conformance Testing Programs).

---

[41] *LFIOS*, State Addendum Question 43. Because most States receive results from the ULW, it may be worthwhile to consider whether or not the ULW should be expanded to include "plug and play" proprietary algorithms for search results and to enable latent examiners to have a consistent graphical user interface across agencies.

[42] *LFIOS*, State Addendum Question 38.

Network Connectivity

The success of law enforcement agencies' coordinated efforts to apprehend suspects of crime across jurisdictional lines depends on the connectivity of different AFIS systems through established networks. Increased connectivity would help overcome the limitations to electronic data sharing that currently exist among local-to-local communications and state-to-state communications. Once technical standards are implemented, current methods of sharing fingerprint image data span from transmitting over electronic secure networks to delivering CDs through the United States Postal Service.

These gaps arose for many of the same reasons that compatibility issues arose. Individual jurisdictions procured AFIS systems from different vendors without consideration of connectivity with other systems within close geographic proximity. Varying privacy laws also prevented States from creating an interconnected network. Where connectivity does exist, it tends to occur in situations where agencies possess AFIS systems from the same vendor. Vendors, in fact, would have a disincentive for local connectivity because it could result in economies of scale that could have a negative financial impact on the industry.

Aside from NGI access, fewer than half of States reported having a direct connection to another law enforcement agency's AFIS system, even though over half of State and local law enforcement agencies reported being part of an AFIS network that contained more than one agency, suggesting that many networks do not permit interoperable data sharing.[43]

Recent Progress on Network Connectivity and Remaining Challenges

Three main networks facilitate the majority of latent print communications among law enforcement agencies: the CJIS-WAN, the International Justice and Public Safety Network (Nlets), and the Law Enforcement Enterprise Portal (LEEP), formerly the Law Enforcement Online network.

Connectivity between the State AFIS systems and NGI is made possible through the CJIS-WAN. Since its adoption the CJIS-WAN has allowed the submission of both ten-prints and latent prints from States to NGI. Most local agencies do not have direct access to NGI, and therefore must contact their State agency

---

[43] *LFIOS*, Questions 242 and 243.

for access. Local agencies that have the ability to directly submit searches against NGI must submit them through LEEP.

Nlets, a not-for-profit organization managed by state-law enforcement agencies, runs a network used to share a wide array of criminal justice and law enforcement information, domestically and internationally. The WIN network and New Hampshire, Maine, and Vermont share interstate latent print information through Nlets.

The FBI's LEEP is an online network used by law enforcement agencies to support investigative operations, to send notifications and alerts, and to provide an avenue to remotely access other law enforcement and intelligence systems and resources. It is not intended to support latent AFIS searches, but developers have created a software wrapper to send emails with attached latent images via LEEP.

None of these systems has the capacity to fully support interoperability among agencies performing latent print searches. The current connectivity system landscape creates major hurdles for connecting agencies both horizontally (locality to locality or State to State) and vertically (locality to State). The CJIS-WAN would require major redesign and redeployment to support extensive local-to-local links, but it may be an alternative for linking States to other States. State agencies are already connected to the FBI through CJIS-WAN and the CJIS Advisory Policy Board has already approved the use of CJIS-WAN to route messages between States. Local agencies may only connect to Nlets through their States' connection, limiting local agencies' ability to make use of the system, and the current system does not support interstate local sharing.

Beginning in June 2017, CJIS will no longer allow local law enforcement agencies to directly access NGI. Direct Latent Connectivity services had been extended to select local law enforcement agencies as an interim solution while States developed the programming and telecommunications infrastructure to support local connectivity for latent services. Advances in technical compatibility are obviating the need for the DLC services. To ensure the continuity of access for local agencies, connected local agencies must work with States to develop and submit a formal Transition Plan to CJIS by December 2014. Once DLC is no longer supported, SIBs will steward additional local connectivity efforts and manage submissions to NGI as is done with other biometric submissions such as ten-prints. The transition process may also help establish a process for SIBs to establish connectivity to additional local agencies.

Overall, in an environment with constrained resources, vertical connectivity will be more feasible than horizontal connectivity across jurisdictions, because agencies could use the existing network infrastructure used for ten-print searches. State-to-State connectivity is of paramount importance, because it will allow for cross-jurisdictional searches that will benefit both State and local law enforcement activities. Connectivity to NGI through LITS-compliant AFIS systems will facilitate State-to-State connectivity.

Once an agency has a LITS-compliant system that is connected to a network, the next step is to facilitate searches against its AFIS. To do so, an agency may make its database more available to searching by registering with CJIS to receive a unique identifier for the Name of Designated Repository (NDR), a field specified in LITS. Once a data sharing MOU is in place, the NDR will facilitate sharing by allowing a law enforcement agency with a LITS-compliant AFIS system to add additional search database destinations into its system, without additional coding.

Path Forward for Network Connectivity

FBI CJIS should work to expand CJIS-WAN to incorporate State-to-State connectivity, because it is already used by other Federal agencies and can handle a large bandwidth. FBI should also look at measures to encourage more agencies to register their AFISs with the NDR so that they may be searched by other jurisdictions in relevant investigations. As more local agencies become LITS-compliant, the FBI could review its policies that restrict local agencies' access to NGI.

For some local jurisdictions, the benefit of local-to-local network connectivity may exceed the current challenges because of the cross-jurisdictional nature of crime in those locations. NIST, NIJ, and CJIS should develop guidelines on how to interconnect interstate and intrastate local jurisdictions.

Proper Governance

Governance agreements create a regulatory framework where cross-jurisdictional latent print searches are routine, standardized, secure, and compliant with relevant privacy policies. Once executed, generally by way of two or more agencies entering into an MOU, agencies with interoperability agreements can securely exchange electronic data within the bounds of privacy laws. By clarifying limits of use and standardizing sharing procedures, information exchange will advance from ad hoc and informal means, to a more profound and integrated collaboration that reflects the complex nature of ensuring public safety today. These governance documents are best used when they are built on the foundation of technical interoperability and network connectivity as discussed above.

The current hierarchical nature of AFIS connectivity means that AFIS systems are integrated more vertically than horizontally and that the potential for horizontal collaboration has yet to be realized. Most local agencies have no formal sharing or governance agreements, even in areas of regional collaboration among States, which is the case for many of the local agencies in the WIN network. An exception is the NOVARIS agreement, which permits regional sharing in the Washington, D.C. area.[44] In response to NIJ's survey, approximately half of State agencies and only a third of local agencies with an AFIS reported having an MOU or service level agreement in place permitting them to use another AFIS.[45] This has resulted in a disparity in search capabilities and efficiencies among and between law enforcement agencies that have AFIS capabilities and a lack of clarity of when it is legal and appropriate to perform multi-jurisdictional searches. AFIS vendors often facilitate the development of MOUs, which means that these relationships often only occur where the agencies involved share the same vendor.

Local and State laws regulate data sharing civil and criminal fingerprint records. Many jurisdictions have policies that preclude the enrollment of ten-prints obtained in a justice setting into another AFIS system if the fingerprints originated from a minor or from an individual convicted of a misdemeanor. Likewise, an agency may limit the retention of fingerprints after a certain period of time. These retention and sharing laws may not be consistent with those of neighboring jurisdictions. Better clarity around existing laws could help local law enforcement agencies develop joint policies that protect civil liberties and respect jurisdictions' preferences for privacy while facilitating sharing among agencies with common criminal pools.

Nationally, many of the privacy concerns are governed by the Federal Privacy Act of 1974 which allows for collection of fingerprints for civil or criminal law enforcement, counterterrorism efforts, and public

---

[44] Even among NOVARIS's partners, examiners must re-encode prints to search their respective State AFIS system and therefore have limited access to the NGI.

[45] *LFIOS*, Question 241.

safety matters. In addition, NGI users must abide by CJIS's security policy regarding "protecting the sources, transmission, storage, and generation of Criminal Justice Information (CJI)."[46]

The FBI's Compact Council, established in 1998 by the National Crime Prevention and Privacy Compact Act, has written rules regarding the collection and use of fingerprints for noncriminal justice purposes (such as application for a job or license, an immigration or naturalization matter, security clearance, or adoption).[47] Further research should be undertaken to assess the extent to which State laws vary in terms of collection of fingerprint data and subsequent use.

Recent Progress on Governance and Remaining Challenges

In order to facilitate more standardized governance agreements, the NIST/NIJ Latent Print AFIS Interoperability Working Group drafted guidelines for developing an MOU between and among agencies that wish to become interoperable.[48] The guidelines include a template for latent print processing agreements between two or more agencies, an overview of how to conduct the process, and sample structure and language for the agreement. The guidelines also provide sample language to address security and privacy disclosures. If an agency adheres to these guidelines, it can produce comprehensive and clear standard operating procedures for cross-jurisdictional latent fingerprint searches.

In addition to the MOU guidelines, the Working Group published a *Glossary of AFIS Terms.*[49] The glossary provides examiners and AFIS users with a comprehensive list of terms associated with AFIS technology. Not only does this glossary allow examiners to communicate more easily with one another using standard terminology, but it also allows others involved with AFIS systems and development, such as procurement officers, vendors, and attorneys, to communicate more clearly.

The FBI is expected to publish a Privacy Impact Assessment on the privacy implications of NGI, including those relevant to latent services. This document is expected to address the additional privacy issues associated with the retention of civil fingerprints and searching those prints against incoming criminal prints.

Path Forward for Proper Governance

In order to encourage the cooperation between and among State and local agencies, NIST should host a workshop or webinar series on how to implement the MOU guidelines. CJIS could develop strategies to coordinate the development of interstate local AFIS governance agreements.

The Department of Justice's Office of Justice Programs could conduct an analysis of State and local privacy laws and other policies related to the retention and use of fingerprints to identify whether and to what extent variability in these policies is serving as a barrier to interoperability.

---

[46] FBI, *Criminal Justice Information Services (CJIS) Security Policy*, (Criminal Justice Information Services, August 4, 2014).

[47] FBI, Compact Council, "Agency Privacy Requirements for Noncriminal Justice Applicants," available at: www.fbi.gov/about-us/cjis/cc/library/agency-privacy-requirements-for-noncriminal-justice-applicants.

[48] Ballou, Susan M.; Garris, Michael D.; Clay, Anthony; Dickerson, Joi; Higgins, Petter T.; Jackson, Lisa; Morrissey, Joe; Owens, Beth; Polski, Joe; Lesko, Mike. Joe Morrissey Norton, Leo, Taylor, Melissa, *Writing Guidelines to Develop an MOU for Interoperable Automated Fingerprint Identification Systems*, NIST Special Publication 1156. (National Institute of Standards and Technology, May 2013).

[49] Latent Print AFIS Interoperability Working Group, *Glossary of AFIS Terms*, (National Institute of Standards and Technology, February 17, 2012).

Performance Testing and Training

Underpinning any interoperable system is the need for assurance that the examiners are adequately trained and the software is compliant with newly adopted standards, provides accurate results, and functions properly. Building in performance testing and training not only helps to maintain the integrity of criminal investigations pursuant to searches, but also serves to advance the field of fingerprinting and biometrics. Additionally, automated solutions must be put in place to assist in the process of combining and sorting candidate lists so that examiners will have the time to follow up on candidate matches as a result of searching other systems. Inherently, the more data searched, the greater the number of candidates returned. Therefore, interoperability will generate a significant amount of work for examiners on the back end to review the increased number of candidates and will require a mechanism to support efficient prioritization and sorting of the many candidates. Moreover, proper training is needed to ensure that examiners are appropriately searching within the bounds of current privacy laws.

Training and Tools

Latent fingerprint examiner training is a critical component of any latent print operation and is also an essential component of AFIS interoperability. Training will become ever more essential as technological upgrades are integrated into AFIS operations. For example, as jurisdictions upgrade their systems to become LITS conformant, latent print examiners will need to receive comprehensive training to ensure they are proficient in the use of the standard EFS markup and in determining which search profile is appropriate to use. Training can also reduce the risk of print comparison error and increase the standardization of the identification process.

In addition to basic fingerprint processing, examiners must be trained in methods for encoding the EFS latent print features and those required for vendor-specific proprietary AFIS database requirements. Unfortunately, there is no universal training program in the field of latent fingerprints. Agencies are typically responsible for designing and implementing their own training programs, and therefore, examiner training varies widely. While most agencies have some certified staff adjudicating candidate lists, most agencies do not require that all examiners be certified.[50] While some training is provided by the vendor, most training is conducted on the job through a mentoring program, with new latent print examiners receiving mentored training by an experienced examiner within the agency. This, in some cases, has resulted in poor quality submissions. For instance, among responding State agencies in the NIJ Survey, one-quarter of States had submissions rejected by the FBI because the submission did not meet the minimum quality standard.[51]

Recent Progress on Training and Remaining Challenges

In order to respond to the demands for standardized training, NIST has developed an EFS online training tool as an interactive guide to latent fingerprint markup.[52] The tool provides an overview on the types of search profiles designated by LITS and allows examiners to practice annotating minutiae.

Further development of training should build on Standard Operating Procedures (SOPs) and conducting proper management and administrative reporting. SOPs complement training programs by improving

---

[50] *LFIOS*, Question 270 and 271.

[51] *LFIOS*, State Addendum Question 40.

[52] The NIST training tool is available at www.nist.gov/forensics/EFSTrainingTool.

examiner performance, staff resource allocation, and examiner expectations. But many latent fingerprint operations do not have documented SOPs around searching other AFIS databases in their agencies.

SOPs should establish a framework for allocating examiner and AFIS resources and should include a policy for determining which searches to make depending on the resources available. The procedures should also outline document requirements for any latent fingerprint identification and should offer policies to mitigate the risk of a print comparison error, the degree of review required, and the review processes based upon levels of comparison difficulty. Finally, the procedures should support the collection and analysis of operations data sufficient for system utilization and upgrade planning (e.g., number of searches made, cases solved, search characteristics, and success factors).

Training materials and programs should include methods for communicating how an examiner processes latent fingerprints in accordance with established and validated SOPs.[53] Communications training will help demonstrate that the latent print comparison is accurate and admissible in court.

Path Forward for Proper Training and Tools

The Federal Government should produce resources to help examiners efficiently and competently perform interoperable searches. To facilitate dissemination of best practices for LITS-compliant systems, NIST should develop guidelines for writing SOPs that incorporate reporting and best practices into the latent print identification process for searches conducted against other agencies' databases. NIJ or Bureau of Justice Assistance (BJA) should introduce grant programs to support examiner training activities related to the implementation and use of LITS/EFS, to mitigate the costs of examiner retraining. In addition to these supporting efforts, NIST should develop guidelines on how examiners might communicate accurate results from a multi-jurisdictional search in testimony and reports.

Just as the FBI has provided the ULW freeware to process NGI search requests, NIST and the FBI should consider developing and making available an automated aggregation tool for candidate lists that are returned from multiple searches in one or more systems when simultaneous searches are appropriate. The tool should able be to prioritize the results and identify the most likely candidate from the combined searches.

Testing

Testing AFIS systems helps ensure that they deliver accurate results while conforming to newly implemented transaction standards. Independent assessment of software performance will help ensure that users understand complex issues that underpin the technical aspects of interoperability and latent print identification. Testing could also be used to optimize examiner workflow, which will help address the increasing examiner demands caused by longer candidate lists as a result of enabling the searching of more AFIS systems. Workflow modifications should be sure to account for the differences in algorithmic weighting that occurs.

Testing has been incorporated into many of the vendors' business models in order to outcompete competitors, but not into law enforcement agencies because of the lack of administrative reporting of search processes and results. Vendors' claims about reliability and accuracy of AFIS identification algorithms, if not independently verified, may be exaggerated to capture market share.

---

[53] The Scientific Working Group on Friction Ridge Analysis, Study and Technology previously developed model Standard Operating Procedures regarding latent print examinations. That can be found at www.swgfast.org/Documents.html

Recent Progress on Testing and Remaining Challenges

Performance testing measures the accuracy of a latent AFIS searches for an AFIS system. Such testing will help ensure that reliability and accuracy objectives are not compromised when implementing interoperable standards. Agencies should require vendors to pass performance tests before accepting a delivered system. Performance testing has yet to be standardized, but the Working Group has identified a few elements that should be included in any performance test. NIST has employed testing to determine interoperability to assess the accuracy of a print encoded on another AFIS system to a natively encoded print.

Path Forward for Testing

To ensure that interoperability standards do not compromise search accuracy, NIST could also consider developing mechanisms to assess the accuracy of a natively or remotely encoded print as well as language to be included in the RFP guidance to ensure high accuracy.

Education and Outreach

The decentralized nature of American law enforcement introduces several challenges with dissemination of pertinent information relating to each of the core elements of interoperability. When standards, resources, policy updates, and training opportunities are adopted, developed, introduced, or announced, not all agencies and relevant stakeholders learn of these developments in a timely manner or at all. In particular, some State and local agencies are not aware of how the newly adopted LITS standard should be implemented, the availability of resources about the standard, or the changes to CJIS search and data retention policies. Education and outreach is an important overarching component for bringing about interoperability.

Following the adoption of the LITS standard, the Interoperability Working Group worked to develop guidelines for the development of MOUs between agencies looking to enter into a latent print sharing agreement and guidelines for appropriate Request for Proposal language to ensure cost-effective LITS-compliance in a new or upgraded AFIS system. Some State and local agencies have not been informed of these resources, jeopardizing the incorporation of LITS into the next generation of AFIS systems across the country and inhibiting interoperability.

When IAFIS was initially introduced, CJIS harbored concerns with exceeding capacity and placed a number of restrictions on what searches could be performed to manage the system. Augmented capacity and the introduction of NGI has enabled CJIS to lift these restrictions. Some State and local agencies maintain the perception that these restrictions are still in place today. This has led to confusion among State and local agencies as to when and under what conditions searches can be performed against NGI. For example, Florida State police were hesitant to search NGI for a suspected drug kingpin charged with Federal crimes who was being held in a local jail. Outreach to local agencies to clarify CJIS's policies should be made a priority to ensure that law enforcement agencies can search NGI when their investigation calls for it.[54]

CJIS staff work closely with individual agencies to evaluate LITS and EBTS implementation in new AFIS systems. An expansion of these efforts could help translate technical specifications into practice by resource-constrained law enforcement agencies seeking to update their systems.

---

[54] FBI, *CJIS Security Policy*.

Summary of Recommendations

The development of standards for latent print encoding and searching (EFS and LITS) is a major step forward in AFIS interoperability. Now the Federal Government must ensure that these systems become the standard by helping State and local agencies build connections across jurisdictions, developing an overall connectivity strategy, fostering better governance, and supporting system-wide quality assurance through testing and training programs.

Interagency Coordination

Establish an interagency group to promote AFIS interoperability standards among Federal, State, and local authorities. This group will also be charged with coordinating and facilitating the development and adoption of standards related to AFIS system use. Coordination of these activities by an interagency group, with cooperation of Federal, State, local, and tribal partners, as well as advice from industry, will help to ensure that users are provided with an integrated suite of standards to support law enforcement and counterterrorism needs. The suite of standards necessary to achieve interoperability and improve efficiency includes standards for evaluating equipment, training and certifying users, accreditation, and development of standard operating procedures.

Technical Compatibility

- All Federal AFIS should be fully standards (LITS) compliant without the use of an additional workstation within 3 years.

- The Federal Government should make the following efforts to encourage the adoption of LITS-compliant AFIS systems by State and local agencies:

  - BJA or NIJ should make funds available through existing grant programs to support State and local agency procurement of LITS-compliant AFIS

  - All Federal funds made available to State and local agencies for AFIS procurement or upgrades should specify that the AFIS system must be LITS-compliant.

- NIST should pursue activities to support the implementation of LITS-compliant AFIS systems through:

  - Periodic review of the recently adopted standards;

  - Ensuring backward compatibility of the standards following any updates; and

  - Ensuring compliance through the development of conformance testing standards and funding conformance testing programs.

Network Connectivity

- FBI CJIS should work to improve State-to-State connectivity by expanding the CJIS-WAN and encouraging more agencies to participate in development of a truly interoperable system.

- FBI CJIS should support local-to-State connectivity and local-to-local connectivity through technical assistance and should also develop with NIST and NIJ guidelines on how to interconnect local jurisdictions.

Governance

- CJIS should develop strategies to coordinate the development of interstate local AFIS governance agreements.

- NIST should host a workshop or webinar series on how to structure interagency agreements that allow for latent print searches that are routine, standardized, secure, and in compliance with relevant privacy policies.

- The Office of Justice Programs should conduct an analysis of State and Federal privacy laws and policies that impact fingerprint sharing across jurisdictions and identify opportunities coordinate the development of joint policies.

Performance Testing and Training

- The Federal Government should support training activities of LITS-compliant systems through the following activities:

    - NIST should develop support materials, including SOPs for examiners.

    - NIJ and BJA should make available funds under current grant programs to support examiner training activities related to the implementation and use of standards-compliant systems.

- NIST could also develop performance tests to assess the matching accuracy of natively versus remotely encoded prints.

- NIST and the FBI could develop and make available an automated tool to aggregate candidate lists from multiple searches in one or more systems that could lead to improvements in efficacy and accuracy.

Education and Outreach

- The Federal Government should help resource-constrained law enforcement agencies seeking to update their systems by expanding efforts to evaluate LITS and EBTS implementation and translate technical specifications into practice.

References

Ballou, Susan M.; Garris, Michael D.; Clay, Anthony; Dickerson, Joi; Higgins, Petter T. ; Jackson, Lisa; Morrissey, Joe; Owens, Beth; Polski, Joe; Lesko, Mike. Joe Morrissey Norton, Leo, Taylor, Melissa. *Writing Guidelines to Develop an MOU for Interoperable Automated Fingerprint Identification Systems. NIST Special Publication* 1156. National Institute of Standards and Technology. May 2013. Accessed July 9, 2014. nvlpubs.nist.gov/nistpubs/SpecialPublications/NIST.SP.1156.pdf.

Federal Bureau of Investigation (FBI). *Electronic Biometric Transmission Specification (EBTS) Technical and Operational Update (TOU) 10.0.2*. (June 2, 2014). Accessed August 21, 2014. www.fbibiospecs.org/docs/EBTS%20TOU%2010_0_2_Final.pdf.

Federal Bureau of Investigation (FBI). "Uniform Crime Report: Crime in the United States, 2012." Fall 2013. Accessed July 7, 2014. www.fbi.gov/about-us/cjis/ucr/crime-in-the-u.s/2012/crime-in-the-u.s.-2012/offenses-known-to-law-enforcement/clearancetopic.pdf.

Federal Bureau of Investigation (FBI). *Privacy Impact Assessment Integrated Automated Fingerprint Identification System (IAFIS)/Next Generation Identification (NGI) Repository for Individuals of Special Concern (RISC)*. July 10, 2012. Accessed September 2, 2014. www.fbi.gov/foia/privacy-impact-assessments/iafis-ngi-risc.

Federal Bureau of Investigation (FBI). *Criminal Justice Information Services (CJIS) Security Policy*. Criminal Justice Information Services, 4 August 4, 2014. Accessed August 22, 2014. www.fbi.gov/about-us/cjis/cjis-security-policy-resource-center/at_download/file.

Federal Bureau of Investigation (FBI). "Agency Privacy Requirements for Noncriminal Justice Applicants." Available at http://www.fbi.gov/about-us/cjis/cc/library/agency-privacy-requirements-for-noncriminal-justice-applicants.

Hicklin, Austin. *Standardizing a More Complete Set of Fingerprint Features.* Noblis, Inc. 2007. Prepared for the Committee to Define to an Extended Feature Set. Accessed 9 July 2014. www.fingerprint.nist.gov/STANDARD/cdeffs/Docs/IAI_CDEFFS_2007-07-24.pdf.

Landon, James J. *Privacy Impact Assessment Integrated Automated Fingerprint Identification System (IAFIS)/Next Generation Identification (NGI) Repository for Individuals of Special Concern (RISC)*. Federal Bureau of Investigation, July 10, 2012. Accessed July 8, 2014. www.fbi.gov/foia/privacy-impact-assessments/iafis-ngi-risc.

Latent Print AFIS Interoperability Working Group. *Glossary of AFIS Terms.* National Institute of Standards and Technology, February 17, 2012.

Latent Print AFIS Interoperability Working Group. *Writing Guidelines for Requests for Proposals for Automated Fingerprint Identification Systems.* National Institute of Standards and Technology, February, 17 2012.

Moses, Kenneth R, Peter Higgins, Michael McCabe, Salil Probhakar, and Scott Swann. "Chapter 6—Automated Fingerprint Identification Systems (AFIS)."In *The Fingerprint Sourcebook*. Washington, D.C.: Department of Justice, 2010, 6-1–33.

National Institute of Standards and Technology (NIST). *Latent Interoperability Transmission Specification*. (NIST Special Publication 1152. January 2013). Accessed July 2014. nvlpubs.nist.gov/nistpubs/SpecialPublications/NIST.SP.1152.pdf.

National Institute of Standards and Technology (NIST). *NIST Special Publication 500-245: Data Format for the Interchange of Fingerprint, Facial, & Scar Mark & Tattoo (SMT) Information*, ANSI/NIST-ITL 1-2000. Washington D.C.: NIST, July 2000.

Noblis, Inc. *Latent Print Interoperability: State and Local Perspectives*. April 2, 2012.

Persinger, Mark, Lars Ericson, and Mark Greene. *Latent Fingerprint Interoperability Survey: A National Study of Automated Fingerprint Information Systems (AFIS) Maintained by Law Enforcement Agencies. Summary Reporting of Data Provided by Responding Agencies.* Washington, D.C.: Department of Justice, August 2014.

National Science and Technology Council

Committee on Science

Subcommittee on Forensic Science

Representatives of Member Departments and Agencies

Department of Commerce

Department of Defense

Department of Energy

Department of Health and Human Services

Department of Homeland Security

Department of Interior

Department of Justice

Department of Treasury

Environmental Protection Agency

National Science Foundation

National Transportation Safety Board

Office of the Federal Public Defender

United States Postal Inspection Service

Smithsonian Institution

Abbreviations

ABIS	Automated Biometric Identification System
AFIS	Automated Fingerprint Identification System
ANSI	American National Standards Institute
BIMA	Biometrics Identity Management Activity
BJA	Bureau of Justice Assistance
CDEFFS	Committee to Define an Extended Fingerprint Feature Set
CJIS	Criminal Justice Information Services
DHS	Department of Homeland Security
DLC	Direct Latent Connectivity
DOD	Department of Defense
EBTS	Electronic Biometric Transmission Standard
EFS	Extended Feature Set
FBI	Federal Bureau of Investigation
IAFIS	Integrated Automated Fingerprint Identification System
IDENT	Automated Biometric Identification System
ITL	Information Technology Laboratory
LITS	Latent Interoperability Transmission Specification
LEEP	Law Enforcement Enterprise Portal, formerly Law Enforcement Online
LFIOS	*Latent Interoperability Transmission Specification*
ME/C	medical examiners and coroners
MOU	memorandum of understanding
NDR	Name of Designated Repository
NGI	Next Generation Identification
NIJ	National Institute of Justice
NIST	National Institute of Standards and Technology
Nlets	National Law Enforcement Telecommunications Systems
NOVARIS	Northern Virginia Regional Identification System
OSTP	Office of Science and Technology Network
RFP	request for proposals
RISC	Repository of Special Concern
SIB	State Identification Bureau
SOP	Standard Operating Procedure

SWGFAST	Scientific Working Group on Friction Ridge Analysis, Study, and Technology
ULF	Unsolved Latent File
ULW	Universal Latent Workstation
US-VISIT	United States Visitor and Immigrant Status Indicator Technology
TXDPS	Texas Department of Public Safety
WAN	Wide Area Network
WIN	Western Identification Network